Photo•Poems

Living Your Best Life,
Even In The Worst Of Times…

Fourth Edition

Draft #8a

Big Thanks To…

Jim Webber and Alison Keithley for poetic consultations; and also
Howard Kimeldorf and Barbara Cooke for editorial input and guidance.

All PhotoArt in this book has been developed by Martin, along with images contributed by the following artists:

Bali, Indonesian Photographer Irine Parini donated her self-portrait for quatrain CV.

PhotoArtist Julie Wagner shared spider webs that were used in the collages
appearing in quatrains CXI and CLVX.

Several images incorporated NASA images found in the public domain,

©.Kimeldorf.2018

Cover art *Flying Fingers* by Martin Kimeldorf

Publishing History: Copyright in 2018 by Martin Kimeldorf.

First Printing First edition April 30, 2018 at Create Space.
It was a full moon and layered with heroic fatalism.

Publication Data: Kimeldorf, Martin.

Photo•Poems   *Living Your Best Life, Even In The Worst Of Times…*

1. Poetry. 2. Photography

Table of Contents

PROLOGUE

In this sixth new title *Photo•Poems*, the author blends his previously published four-line quatrains with his award winning PhotoArt. Martin's poems are inspired by Edward FitzGerald's interpretation of the enduring verse found in *The Rubaiyat of Omar Khayyam*. The result is a very readable and engaging volume that celebrates the life we have left, and poses fundamental questions about the search for meaning in difficult times.

Martin has learned from the inventive poets, scientists, artists and thinkers, who came before and urged us to remain skeptical of dogma and convention, especially fundamentalism of any stripe. Like them, he believes humor and doubt are critical survival tools in these turbulent times. To that end, he deploys the comedic devices of irony and satire when reflecting on that peculiar journey we call life. In Quatrain VII he writes:

> *There's no cure for being born human,*
>
> *we create our own pain deep within...*
>
> *Tease yourself to survive your Self.*
>
> *Laugh often to avoid ending broken.*

Join the author in contemplating the mysterious, star-filled cosmos. Ponder it long enough and you may glimpse the heavens winking back, and hear a soft chuckle.

This book draws heavily on the heroic fatalism first espoused in the earlier Stoic, Socratic, Epicurean and Buddhist philosophies. You can also find these thoughts threaded throughout the *Rubáiyát*. Come lift a glass of your favorite beverage as you toast our unknown destinies—as we try to embrace the joy of seizing the day before us.

GENESIS

My father Don was an avid collector and organizer of all kinds of hardware. His workbench backed up to a wall of fasteners, tools, and electrical gizmos, all neatly sorted and labeled. He also collected his sons' lifelong attempts at self-expression. In my case, this included a stash of letters, home-made cards, poems, plays, published works, report cards, and various artifacts. (Apparently, when I was five year old I picked up a hammer and screw driver, and then pounded a stick-figure-story into a piece of soft pine.) And when I turned 50, he returned this first attempt at wood-based story telling.

My early wood-carved-story

A year later, inspired by the early wood-carved-story, my mother Fay carpooled me over to San Carlos to enroll in painting classes. Everyone seemed to fuss over my primitive and colorful attempts. The cover on this book contains a "self-portrait" done in that early primitive style, but completed in my 40s.

My father was also a lifelong amateur photographer and scrapbook keeper. Unlike the sterile scrapbooks of the time with neatly organized rows of images and captions, my dad would cut out photos in artful ways, and then creatively display them with humorous comments. He sometimes glued images together into artistic collages. Finally, in our early teens Don installed a dark room. Out of these experiences my brothers and I developed an enduring interest in photography. In the 1990s I returned to photography and began exploring the emerging digital darkroom.

I begin my painting life at 6.

From Film to Digital Pictorialism

Around 2004 I earned enough through writing to buy my first digital camera. The amazing computer tools provided an unparalleled set of options compared to the wet darkrooms of the film era. I could see the painterly-photographic possibilities first advocated by a group known as the Pictorialists.

The Pictorialists emerged in the second half of the 19ᵗʰ Century in reaction to the camera's mechanical or overly-literal capture of the subject. Inspired by popular impressionistic styles trending through the painters' world, their goal was nothing short of reinventing photography. Many of their admirers claimed that Pictorialism gave the camera "poetic" wings.

Fueled by their energy and vision, I began by creating multi-layered digital images. Each individual layer contained its own painterly style. Then I hand-blended the layers together with the goal of creating a digital painting, or what I then called *PhotoArt*. Today's magical digital tools enable all of us to fully realize the Pictorialists' dream. As the new century dawned, I began to connect digital Pictorialism with journaling online in a work entitled *Digital Photo Journal.*

My Poetic Inclinations

In 1948, the year I was born, my mother gave my dad the ever-popular poetry book *The Rubáiyát of Omar Khayyám.* My father would often recite Omar's poems, or quatrains, out loud. This instilled in me a similar love for the poetry.

In 2013, I was stopped in my tracks by an *Annus Horribilis*—Latin for *Horrible Year.* In that year, I faced four assaults on my existence, culminating in the removal of a brain tumor. To prepare for each medical "adventure," and to calm my jittery soul, I returned to reading the philosophical and ironic verse contained in *The Rubáiyát of Omar Khayyám.* I found refuge in the quatrain's lyrical, joyful, and mystical fatalism. Surviving that dark night of my soul placed me onto a reflective path lit by expanding insight. I set out to explore more deeply the themes found in Omar's verse: mortality, love, living in the moment, sensuality, drink and fatalism. Today, some 70+ years later, I still enjoy reading those same poems aloud and now write my own quatrains.

The original poems in *The Rubáiyát of Omar Khayyám* were written during the Middle Ages by a Persian polymath who excelled at astronomy, mathematics, calendar design, philosophy and obviously writing. About 6000 kilometers away, and some 600 years later, the Victorian bohemian Edward FitzGerald would emerge as his world-famous English interpreter. These poetic soul-brothers are often referred to as the FitzOmars. Like many creative geniuses throughout the ages, Omar and FitzGerald doubted the inherited truths and conventions of their age. The dynamic duo questioned religious pieties and dogma of all kinds.

Recent scholarship suggests that Khayyám wrote his poems as an after-thought, or perhaps for entertainment in the royal court, or while drinking with his friends. His fatalistic, symbolic and exuberant quatrains encourage us to "Make the most of what we may yet spend, before we too into the dust descend." The poems celebrate the joy of wine, the power of love, and accepting Fate's ironic whimsy. The FitzOmars encourage independent thought, living in the moment, and performing compassionate acts. I found their comedic-tragic view of life prescribed the best way to understand our brief existence.

The FitzOmars' poetry also resonates deeply within today's troubling epoch. The books about their lives and poetry expand our present perspective by describing earlier times when communities were also being torn apart by demagogues; and when fundamentalists, rulers and militarists preached fear and hatred. They too witnessed how authoritarian elites tried to squash democratic impulses.

As a result, their rhymed-thoughts can help us find meaning, courage, and possibly some hope in our darkening moment. The FitzOmars bequeath us many poetic lessons for living our best life in trying times. The following quatrain acknowledges the fragility of our temporary existence.

> The Moving Finger writes; and, having writ,
> Moves on: nor all thy Piety nor Wit
> Shall lure it back to cancel half a Line,
> Nor all thy Tears wash out a Word of it.

Then they raise their cups of forgetfulness and urge us to relish the present opportunities for happiness…

> Come, fill the Cup, and in the Fire of Spring
> The Winter Garment of Repentance fling:
> The Bird of Time has but a little way
> To fly-- and Lo! the Bird is on the Wing.

The FitzOmars (and those writing in their spirit) set out to anchor their personal truths within their own poems. They view the horizon with a satirical grin, then invite us to envision an alternative future.

> Ah Love! could thou and I with Fate conspire
> To grasp this sorry Scheme of Things entire,
> Would not we shatter it to bits -- and then
> Re-mould it nearer to the Heart's Desire.

The poem's spirit of joy and longing belong to every age, to every thoughtful generation trying to find a path to a fulfilling life in challenging times. I use their comedic-tragic view of life to gather the maximum satisfaction from my all-to-brief existence. Perhaps this is why *The Rubáiyát of Omar Khayyám* has outsold all other poetry books in the history of modern publishing.

Completing My FitzOmar Apprenticeship

In 2015 I began a deep dive into the lives of these two poets, their historical times, and the meaning behind their poems or quatrains. I discovered that *The Rubáiyát of Omar Khayyám* was not only the most published and quoted English-language poem in in the world, but it also has become the most illustrated book of poems. In 2016 I blended some of my personal story with my research notes in a new title *Sipping From The Rubaiyat's Chalice*.

Upon finishing that booklet, I rewarded myself by purchasing the out-of-print, comprehensive, and insightful book *The Art of Omar Khayyám* by William Martin and Sandra Mason. This art-poetry-history book masterfully penetrated the meaning of the *Rubáiyát* in ways I had not fully grasped. This ignited an exploding star in my brain during April's birthday month. Many days my eyes fluttered open from a dream at about 4:00 AM. In those early hours I heard the sounds of rhymed phrases or glimpsed a Pictorialist-like visual image. As the morning light slowly chased away the night, I tried to capture these dream-sourced quatrains on my iPhone's notepad; then revised with a digital thesaurus and rhyming dictionary.

In that mystical month, out poured almost 60 of my own quatrains inspired by Martin and Mason's book. I chose to illustrate my contemporary quatrains mainly with pet photos and photomontages under a new title *Kibble for the Soul* in 2017. Like my FitzOmar brethren, I tried to *re-mould the world* closer to my desires for a kinder world. I would then spend most of 2018 adding new poems and revising older ones until I assembled over 170 quatrains. That next April the muse returned to suggest pairing earlier PhotoArt with my favorite quatrains. Now this earlier journey, inspired by the Pictorialists and FitzOmars, is nearing its completion with this *Photo•Poems* booklet.

Following the Photo•Poem Roadway

While the *Kibbles* book was limited to black and white images, this one features full color photo-and-word collages. Sometimes that makes the words hard to highlight or leaves little room to write reactions on the page. Therefore, each photomontage is followed on the next page by the verse alone. Hopefully the white space calls out to you, asking you to adapt a line to two for your own uses, pen a comment, or write your own extension for the quatrain. You will also find brief commentary before each chapter, and I've included two cocktail recipes. All poems are titled or numbered with Roman

Numerals as in the tradition of *The Rubáiyát of Omar Khayyám*. The number indicates the order in which it was written.

Over the years various people have toyed with how to sequence or group quatrains. I have chosen to group my verse around shared themes. Since no one poem is limited to a single theme, consider the groupings as temporary or fluid.

Part I opens upon a cup of love, defined in the broadest way possible. Part II highlights the value of humor in troubled times, and then fans out across topical and religious complaints, ending with thoughts about our tool-making skills and digital evolutions. Part III explores different ways to express heroic fatalism and my overall Omarian worldview. Part III also includes my distinctly un-Omarian view that we are part of a larger continuity that extends beyond our individual mortal existence. And the final chapter bids you farewell or adios.

I hope you enjoy this collection of images and words. Placed on your coffee table, it will hopefully warm and entertain you before an autumn fire. Alternately, lay it at your bed side, or turn the pages in a favorite summer cocktail chair. Book in hand, gently sip, reflect, and peer beneath the surface of this life.

*My father and I
collaged before scrapbooks.
Circa 1980s, Corvallis, Oregon*

PART I—SIPPING FROM A CUP OF LOVE

In this section the FitzOmarDorfs gather to raise their cup of love in a toast to life's many pleasures. This *love cup* celebrates romantic gestures, familial recollections, feelings for our pets, and versifying about working, playing and aging. And threaded across the canvas is the love of learning. Come, elevate your spirit as you salute life with a cocktail or favorite beverage held high

When you're lucky enough to sip from a cup of love, much of life seems like a satisfying dream come true in that moment. Drinking from a chalice of spirits, while reciting a poem or two, can also provide an escape from the blues. Sipping and reflecting on our blessings helps us to accept the hand fate has dealt us. We toast to celebrate our survival, arrival, or departures. Hopefully, Part I melodically trumpets the call to *Carpe Diem—Seize the Day!*

Their looks, poses, greetings—always mine.
My most devoted friends, forever canine!
Stroking their soft coat soothes my anxious heart,
I taught them tricks—my furry Einsteins.

IV

Their looks, poses, greetings—always mine.
My most devoted friends, forever canine!
Stroking their soft coat soothes my anxious heart,
I taught them tricks—my furry Einsteins.

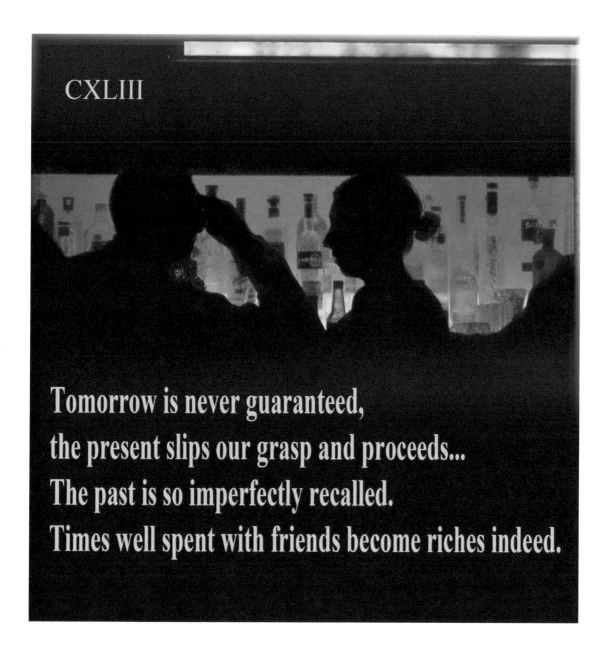

CXLIII

Tomorrow is never guaranteed,
the present slips our grasp and proceeds...
The past is so imperfectly recalled.
Times well spent with friends become riches indeed.

CXLIII

Tomorrow is never guaranteed,

the present slips our grasp and proceeds...

The past is so imperfectly recalled.

Times well spent with friends become riches indeed.

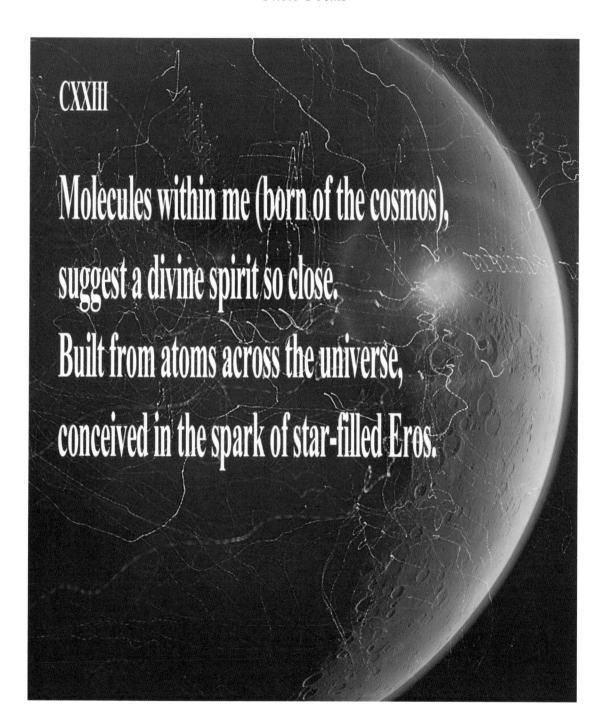

CXXIII

Molecules within me (born of the cosmos),

suggest a divine spirit so close.

Built from atoms across the universe,

conceived in the spark of star-filled Eros.

CXXIII

Molecules within me (born of the cosmos),

suggest a divine spirit so close.

Built from atoms across the universe,

conceived in the spark of star-filled Eros.

CLVIII

All week I've traded words for tears, again.

Guess it's time to change my lyrics, again.

I'll keep moving to find my balance, again.

When I know what to say I'll talk, again.

CLVIII

All week I've traded words for tears, again.

Guess it's time to change my lyrics, again.

I'll keep moving to find my balance, again.

When I know what to say I'll talk, again.

Our cosmos is filled with dark emptiness.
Our final test: the void's mute godlessness.
Pour your song, poem, and drink into the glass,
and find your way into love's warming caress.

CV

Our cosmos is filled with dark emptiness.

Our final test: the void's mute godlessness.

Pour your song, poem, and drink into the glass,

and find your way into love's warming caress.

Where is Cupid, he has broken my heart?

Why has he left me a world both cold and dark!

Toss the peanuts and bring me a stiff drink...

Amidst stupid ones, loving you keeps me smart.

L

Where is Cupid, he has broken my heart?

Why has he left me a world both cold and dark!

Toss the peanuts and bring me a stiff drink...

Amidst stupid ones, loving you keeps me smart

My Judy Valentine Quatrain CLIV (154)

When we're born a clock begins deep inside...
It ticks so sweetly with you by my side.
Time is richly felt with your hand in mine.
I smile, reminisce, and grow misty-eyed...

CLIV

When we're born a clock begins deep inside...

It ticks so sweetly with you by my side.

Time is richly felt with your hand in mine.

I smile, reminisce, and grow misty-eyed...

Quatrain LXXXV

**Mother's Day or Father's Day,
Birth of days…**

Time slips away, taking us too long to say,

**"You've made me ready for the world."
Forever cherishing how I was raised.**

LXXXV

Mother's Day or Father's Day, Birth of days…

Time slips away, taking us too long to say,

"You've made me ready for the world."

Forever cherishing how I was raised.

CLII

Only with affection can we thrive,
as we tease destiny to survive.
Master this tango on the cliff's edge,
dance with both highs and lows to feel alive.

CLII

Only with affection can we thrive,

as we tease destiny to survive.

Master this tango on the cliff's edge,

dance with both highs and lows to feel alive.

CLXX

As thunder rattles the sky,
stand with me....

When the clock slows
and time begins to flee....

then Sit with me,
Be with me,
Stand by me...

and keep close the story
of my debris.

CLXX

As thunder rattles the sky, stand with me....

When the clock slows and time begins to flee....

then Sit with me, Be with me, Stand by me...

and keep close the story of my debris.…..

XXI

We can never grasp the mystery entire.
What is certain, we live and then expire.
Praise not the fool's riddles, nor the many rules,
Rather, grasp a jug, flower, and love's fire.

XXI

We can never grasp the mystery entire.

What is certain, we live and then expire.

Praise not the fool's riddles, nor the many rules,

Rather, grasp a jug, flower, and love's fire.

Blue Moon Pineapple Martini 2018

Blue Moons are few and far between, representing 2 moons in a single month. On January 31, 2018 we had the trifecta of lunar events: a blue moon, super moon, and lunar eclipse. It was time for a blue moon party.

In a large shaker with ice put per drink:

1 part vodka

¼ part Blue Curacao

½ part lime cordial (this is an approximation amount, you may want to add to taste)

½ part pineapple juice

Shake it up and then pour the elixir into a martini glass.

Top it off with a slight squeeze of a lemon wedge, and leaving the fruit in the glass.

CXV

Don't repent, they can't
hear you after death.

Spend all that you can,
before your last breath!

The past was used, the
future beyond reach—

Drain your cup until
nothing is left.

CXV

Don't repent, they can't hear you after death.

Spend all that you can, before your last breath!

The past was used, the future beyond reach—

Drain your cup until nothing is left.

We plot, waver, then
move our chess piece—

Surprised we land on
the square of caprice!

Plan all you want but
fate plays with a whim,

never our destiny can
we police.

CLV

We plot, waver, then move our chess piece—

Surprised we land on the square of caprice!

Plan all you want but fate plays with a whim,

never our destiny can we police.

Make Your Move Cocktail Poem

Here is a new FitzOmarian drink to sip when you want to toast your fate, your choices, and the fact that you only live once. A full bodied, delightful sweet-sour citrussy 'fizz'.

1.5 oz. Gin

½ oz. Roses Lime Juice

1 oz. fresh squeezed orange juice (about half orange)

½ oz. Pamplemousse

1 oz. Soda

Add a few ice cubes…

XCVII

Too quickly we spill from day into night.
What came before, what comes after...What might?
Briefly enjoy the cup of sweet, sweet life,
Empty the glass and toast being finite.

XCVII

Too quickly we spill from day into night.

What came before, what comes after...What might?

Briefly enjoy the cup of sweet, sweet life,

Empty the glass and toast being finite.

XLIX

If we stop playing, age comes fast and cold
unconsciously trading young for old.
We weep for time so quickly passing,
Slowing down turns our free time into gold.

XLIX

If we stop playing, age comes fast and cold
unconsciously trading young for old.
We weep for time so quickly passing,
Slowing down turns our free time into gold.

CLXXII

The eyelash blinks
and time quickly slips bye...

Today joins yesterday's
legion of sighs.

As liquid dreams glide
through the hourglass,

Tomorrow leans in to
whisper,
"Sooo-Prize!"

CLXXII

The eyelash blinks and time quickly slips bye...

Today joins yesterday's legion of sighs.

As liquid dreams glide through the hourglass,

Tomorrow leans in to whisper, "Sooo-Prize!"

XXXVI

Behind the wheel I wailed my blues!
Out of tune I spread the good news.
Blowing my blues harp mostly alone,
this I must Play, my soul to Amuse.

XXXVI

Behind the wheel I wailed my blues!

Out of tune I spread the good news.

Blowing my blues harp mostly alone,

this I must Play, my soul to Amuse.

LXXXVIII

She did not know what to be at twenty-five.
She was confounded by turning forty-five.
At sixty she asked "What next could I be?"
growing up seems to take an eternity...

LXXXVIII

She did not know what to be at twenty-five.
She was confounded by turning forty-five.
At sixty she asked "What next could I be?"
growing up seems to take an eternity...

CXXIX

Born in the baby booming golden age,

hitchhiked towards dream-filled stars

beyond the page.

Did we make a difference?
Who can tell?

Brooding we retire
from the main stage.

CXXIX

Born in the baby booming golden age,

hitchhiked towards dream-filled sky beyond the page.

Did we make a difference? Who can tell?

Brooding we retire from the main stage.

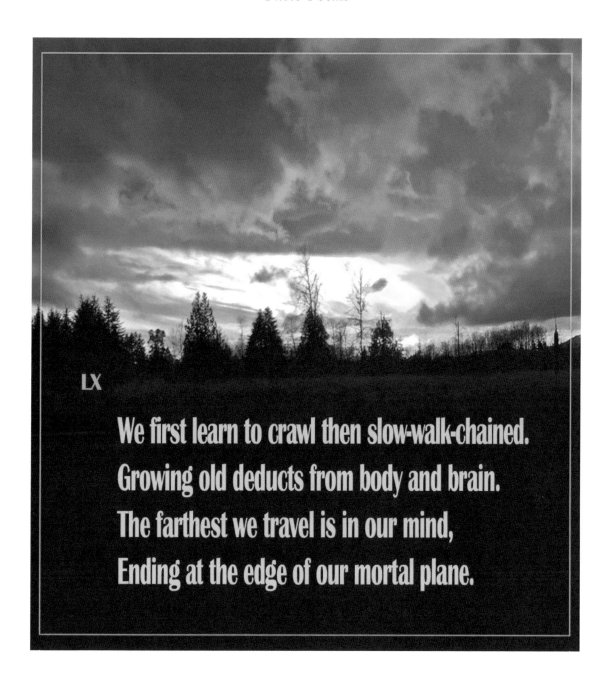

LX

We first learn to crawl then slow-walk-chained.
Growing old deducts from body and brain.
The farthest we travel is in our mind,
Ending at the edge of our mortal plane.

LX

We first learn to crawl then slow-walk-chained.

Growing old deducts from body and brain.

The farthest we travel is in our mind,

Ending at the edge of our mortal plane.

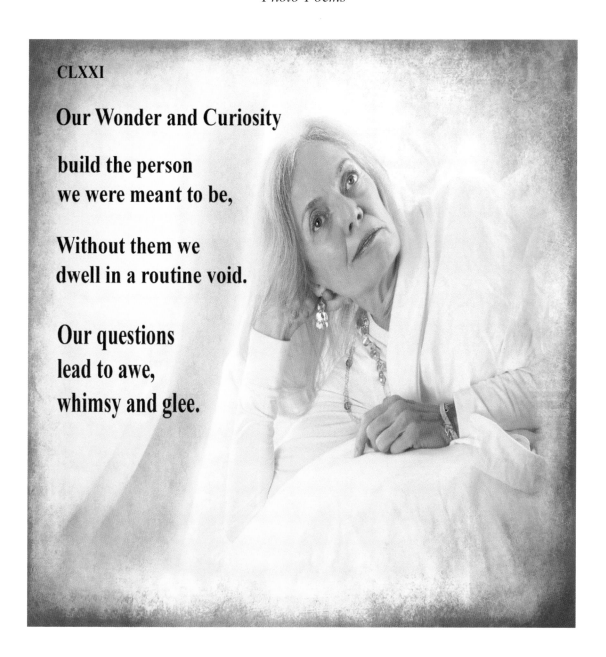

CLXXI

Our Wonder and Curiosity

build the person
we were meant to be,

Without them we
dwell in a routine void.

Our questions
lead to awe,
whimsy and glee.

CLXXI

Our Wonder and Curiosity
build the person we were meant to be,
Without them we dwell in a routine void.
Questions open to Awe, whimsy and glee.

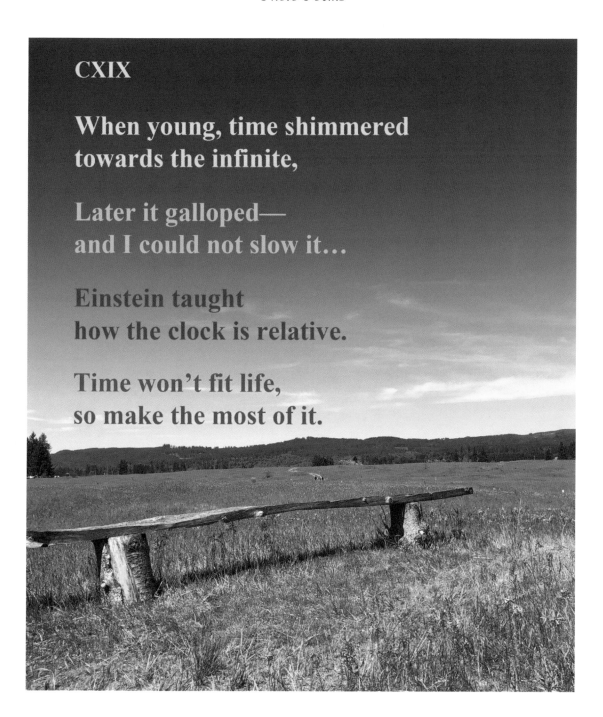

CXIX

**When young, time shimmered
towards the infinite,**

**Later it galloped—
and I could not slow it…**

**Einstein taught
how the clock is relative.**

**Time won't fit life,
so make the most of it.**

CXIX

When young, time shimmered towards the infinite,

Later it galloped—and I could not slow it…

Einstein taught how the clock is relative.

Time won't fit life, so make the most of it.

PART II—IRONY AND SKEPTICISM

Part II deploys the devices of humor, satire, and paradox to make meaning out of our history, contemporary society, and future hopes. This involves versifying about topical current affairs and poking fun at our so-called tool-making prowess (e.g. atomic bombs, addictive smart phones, and miraculous medicines).

Across my life I remain the doubter. Like the FitzOmars, I ask too many questions that are often punctuated with ironic chuckles. And, no matter how much I study, I always come around to Socrates' point of view: "I only know at this point in my life I still don't know." Along this route, many lines in this chapter carve their way through the ancient-yet-modern truth: *there is no cure for being human*. Let me sum up the benefit of humor in my studies with these two lines:

> *Sip from a jug of laughter to survive.*
> *Self-deprecating words keep us alive.*

In Pursuit of A Balanced Epicurean, Stoic, Skeptical Life
Many Greek philosophers believed that the pursuit of "pleasure" leads to the pursuit of the greatest good—but only when one lives modestly and compassionately. In a similar vein, the FitzOmars would later point out that both heaven and hell can emerge from the singular pursuit of pleasure at all costs. They wrote the following lines with this in mind.

> *Heav'ns but the Vision of fulfill'd Desire*
> *And hell the Shadow from a Soul on fire.*

The followers of Zeon (Stoicism), Plato, Socrates and Epicurus shunned the singular pursuit of pleasure that leads only to self-centered hedonistic, narcissistic, or exclusively materialistic ends. This is why Socrates and Epicurus shunned wealth, power, and fame—refusing to charge fees for teaching. Socrates conducted classes barefoot to emphasize the value of the simple and contemplative life. His fellow truth-seeker, Epicurus admitted both women and slaves into his classrooms. He too rejected the materialistic lifestyle—avoiding gourmet gluttony by eating the same simple food each day.

FitzOmar followers promote a temperate lifestyle while enjoying a cups of love and wine. At the same time, they seek a modest balance. In more practical terms it means searching for a golden mean between pleasures with others and service to others.

The Temptation of Franky

There's no cure for being born human,
we create our own pain deep within…
Tease yourself to survive your Self.
Laugh often to avoid ending broken.

VII

There's no cure for being born human,
we create our own pain deep within…
Tease yourself to survive your Self.
Laugh often to avoid ending broken.

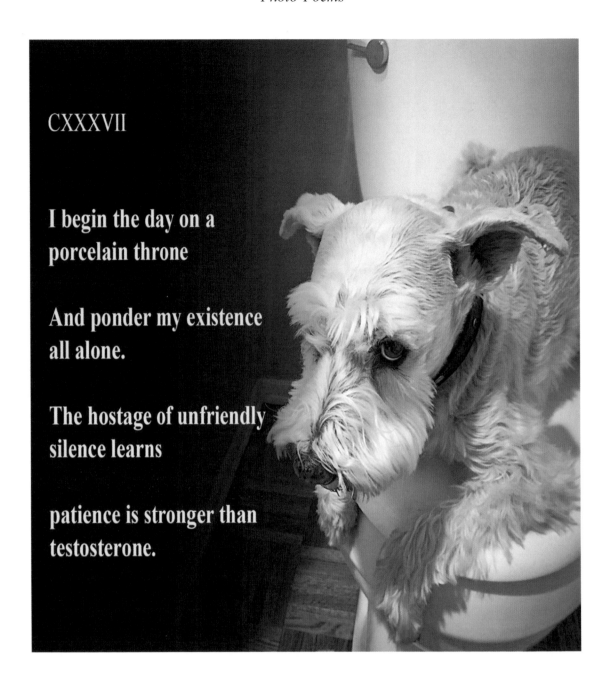

CXXXVII

I begin the day on a
porcelain throne

And ponder my existence
all alone.

The hostage of unfriendly
silence learns

patience is stronger than
testosterone.

CXXXVII

I begin the day on a porcelain throne
And ponder my existence all alone.
The hostage of unfriendly silence learns
patience is stronger than testosterone.

VIII

Sip from a jug of laughter to survive,
Self-deprecating words keep us alive.
To stay limber, grin like a yogi, then
laugh at your fate—and you'll be revived.

VIII

Sip from a jug of laughter to survive,

Self-deprecating words keep us alive.

To stay limber, grin like a yogi, then

laugh at your fate—and you'll be revived.

CX—MY THANK-YOU QUATRAIN

I sit with my books on the sidewalk,
across the empty cement, I then chalk:
"Will write for food, amusement, and comments…"
With your kind words, my calling I unlock.

CX

I sit with my books on the sidewalk,

across the empty cement, I then chalk:

"Will write for food, amusement, and comments…"

With your kind words, my calling I unlock.

VI

Thoughts too serious means too many pills.

Then I learned to laugh to survive my ills.

Shadows still fall, yet I remain upright,

as laughter heals—then fewer doctor bills.

VI

Thoughts too serious means too many pills.

Then I learned to laugh to survive my ills.

Shadows still fall, yet I remain upright,

as laughter heals—then fewer doctor bills.

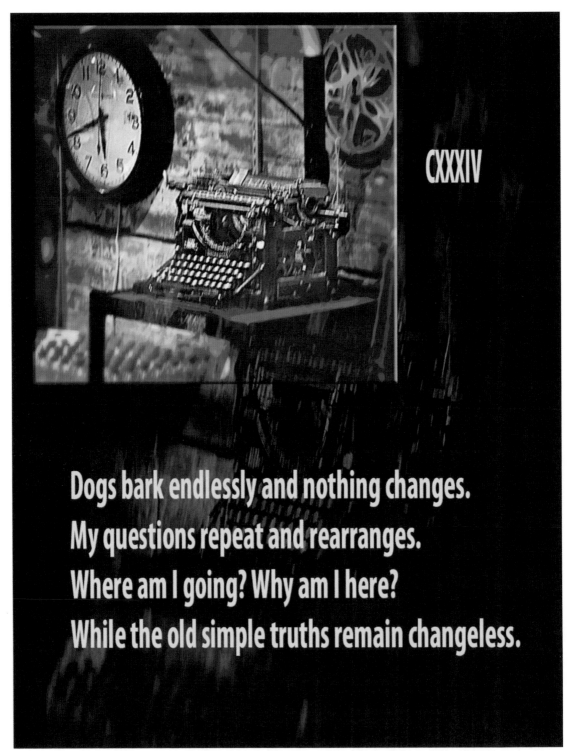

CXXXIV

Dogs bark endlessly and nothing changes.
My questions repeat and rearranges.
Where am I going? Why am I here?
While the old simple truths remain changeless.

CXXXIV

Dogs bark endlessly and nothing changes.

My questions repeat and rearranges.

Where am I going? Why am I here?

While the old simple truths remain changeless.

XCVIX

Hold the utopian eccentrics close
breathe in the warm light of the dreamer's prose.
Tyrants must stifle your hopes and ideals…
Dreams can stop this darkness as fear is deposed.

XCIX

Hold the utopian eccentrics close

breathe in the warm light of the dreamer's prose.

Tyrants try to stifle hopes and ideals…

Dreams can stop this darkness as fear is deposed.

An American Obituary

July 4, 1776

Nov. 8, 2016

XXIII

The population bomb burst so very distinct,

Climate change, mushroom cloud—can't act or think,

Donald Trump-ed our bets on the future...

Homo Sapiens on sale— since going extinct.

XXIII

The population bomb burst so very distinct,

Climate change, mushroom cloud—can't act or think,

Donald Trump-ed our bets on the future...

Homo Sapiens on sale— since going extinct.

CLXXIV

When the word WE is replaced
by the ME,

our own hands
destroy
the community.

Empires rise briefly
only
to collapse;

Tell me—what were we meant
to truly be.

CLXXIV

When the word WE is replaced by the ME,

our own hands destroy the community.

Empires rise briefly only to collapse;

Tell me—what were we meant to truly be.

CXVIII

They're turning abandoned missile silos
into lavish apocalyptic condos.
Condemned to solitary confinement...
Survival of the fittest--bravo!

CXVIII

**They're turning abandoned missile silos
into lavish apocalyptic condos.
Condemned to solitary confinement…
Survival of the fittest—bravo!**

CLXII

What has our Omnipotent God forgot?
Would the perfect potter create cracked pots?
Why does God need a mullah, rabbi, priest…
but to gloss over the two-faced dry rot.

A Spiritual Atheist's Verse...

CLXIII

As people adopt the bully's right,
hate-filled voices rage against the light.
Using God's dogma they crush common sense,
plunging our history into darkest night.

CLXIV

Standing awe-struck before the sky's invite
I sense an infinite knowing light.
While religion is God's greatest failure—
"Doing for others" is a God-like insight.

CLXII

What has our Omnipotent God forgot?
Would the perfect potter create cracked pots?
Why does God need a mullah, rabbi, priest…
but to gloss over the two-faced dry rot.

CLXIII

As people adopt the bully's right,
hate-filled voices rage against the light.
Using God's dogma they crush common sense,
plunging our history into darkest night.

CLXIV

Standing awe-struck before the sky's invite
I sense an infinite knowing light.
While religion is God's greatest failure—
"Doing for others" is a God-like insight.

CIV

Tool-making species crafted love and fire
with Venus and Sisyphus we did conspire.
Made a sacred suicide pact for escape,
Our gifts now heaven's greatest satire.

CIV

Tool-making species crafted love and fire;

with Venus and Sisyphus we did conspire.

Promising holy suicide for escape,

Our gifts now heaven's greatest satire.

CXXVIII

Tune in—Turn off the Notifications!

Restore real human communications...

Don't let the little screen steal your life,

make feelings and laughter the new fixation.

CXXVII

Tune in—Turn off the Notifications!
Restore real human communications…
Don't let the little screen steal your life,
make feelings and laughter the new fixation.

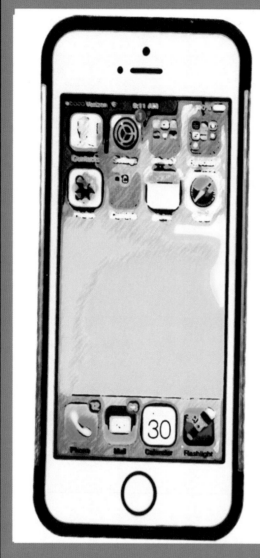

XCIV

You can't seize the day
with glass screen in hand,

It takes you to a fragile
nowhere land.

It's not a substitute for
what is real!

Log off to touch the
enchanted and grand!

XCIV

You can't seize the day with glass screen in hand,

It takes you to a fragile nowhere land.

It's not a substitute for what is real!

Log off to touch the enchanted and grand!

CXLIX

Stardust evolves as self-aware matter,
then remakes itself searching for answers.
Half-aware it heads towards self-extinction.
Stars wonder, "Do humans really matter?"

CXLIX

Stardust evolves as self-aware matter,

then remakes itself searching for answers.

Half-aware it heads towards self-extinction.

Stars wonder, "Do humans really matter?"

PART III—HEROIC FATALISM & COSMIC CONTINUITY

Early cultures embraced a fatalistic view of life, believing that we suffer less when we accept what fate places at our feet. In the Greco-Roman societies they blended fatalism into philosophies of stoicism, epicurean quests, and Socratic dialogues. Their forms of fatalism were never intended to condone being apathetic, withdrawn, or self-centered. In fact, the ultimate form of acceptance becomes what I call *heroic fatalism*.

When Chief Low Dog rode into the Battle of Little Bighorn he demonstrated his heroic fatalism. He turned to the other braves, let out a war whoop and yelled back, "This is a good day to die. Follow me." Not all heroic acts are this dangerous or exceptional.

Writing in the *Baltimore Sun* Meredith Cohn described John O'Malley's laudable odyssey. He enjoyed a rich and long career as a high-ranking federal official. Unexpectedly, he had to take an early retirement after his wife was diagnosed with cancer in 2005. And after she passed away, he was so impressed with the empathic nursing care that he decided to take the training necessary to become a hospice nurse. Cohn reported how O'Malley often stayed past his shift to bring companionship to those with few visitors. When he finally left his work for the day, he always felt like he had done some good in this world. The reporter ended her interview by asking him how long he would keep at his self-appointed task. O'Malley ironically replies, "I'll probably stop when they bring out a bed for me."

Everyday people like O'Malley understand deep down in their bones Omar's lines about the moving finger of time writing, moving on—and how not a single line of it can be cancelled. People like O'Malley accept their fate or destiny by filling up their cup of emptiness with compassion, romantic idealism and heroic efforts.

Mortality and Continuity

We can also glimpse a deeper purpose in our lives and our fate as we mull over this temporary assignment we call *life*. Ironically, pondering death elevates the importance of our remaining time to live. This meditation invites us to speculate on where we might have been before being born, and where our essence might go after we die.

The Greek philosophers and the FitzOmar crew doubted the existence of heaven and hell. And yet, these poets and philosophers refused to succumb to the fear of death while they lived. In particular, Khayyám and Fitzgerald preferred to make the most of the years they had been given. They robustly seized the opportunities for living each day to its fullest.

Though we are here but briefly, I believe our existence belongs to a timeless story. I sense we were all part of something before we were born and will return to that "something" after we leave our mortal shell behind. Some call this notion reincarnation. Others refer to the law of thermodynamics which describes how matter cannot be destroyed nor created; it only changes form. Perhaps it is merely cosmic re-cycling. In my *Kibbles for the Soul* book I called this the *Cosmic Continuity*. In the end, I'm not sure our limited brains will ever be able to fully understand the larger tapestry, and the threads that bind us into the larger picture.

I only know this truth through personal studies and experience. I trust my intuition on this one. I can't prove it—I don't need to.

For me, the sense of a cosmic continuity does not conflict with the FitzOmar brand of fatalism, where our destiny remains ever changing and unknowable. Today, more than ever, I often hear the call to seize happiness in the present moment, rather than delaying or waiting for a future that may never come. I can simultaneously embrace both carpe diem and cosmic continuity with arms wide open.

XXVIII

Heaven weeps and falls from the sky—all too soon.
We'll never carry our sad story beyond the Moon.
God stop this blood-soaked race from poisoning the stars—
The cosmos looks away, our existence impugned.

XXVIII

Heaven weeps and falls from the sky—all too soon.

We'll never carry our sad story beyond the Moon.

God stop this blood-soaked race from poisoning the stars—

The cosmos retreats, our existence impugned.

CVII

Firmly make your move
within the flow.
The edge of the board
comes quickly
... you know.

The checkerboard
has no in-between grays—
We come, travel quickly
...then must go.

CVII

Firmly make your move within the flow.

The edge of the board comes quickly... you know.

The checkerboard has no in-between grays—

We come, travel quickly...then must go.

CXIII

The Spirit is spirit, all else just dirt.

Time seems endless, until we grow alert.

Inhale schemes and dreams to sail far beyond...

After blowing away we feel no hurt.

CXIII

The Spirit is spirit, all else just dirt.

Time seems endless, until we grow alert.

Inhale schemes and dreams to sail far beyond...

After blowing away we feel no hurt.

C

My first and only part in a play,
Much Ado About Nothing

As fate pens your part
on a hidden page,

fiercely play your brief scene
upon the stage.

Pause in the wings
and you've waited too long,

In the final act
you must exit downstage...

C

As fate pens your part on a hidden page,

fiercely play your brief scene upon the stage.

Pause in the wings and you've waited too long,

In the final act you exit downstage…

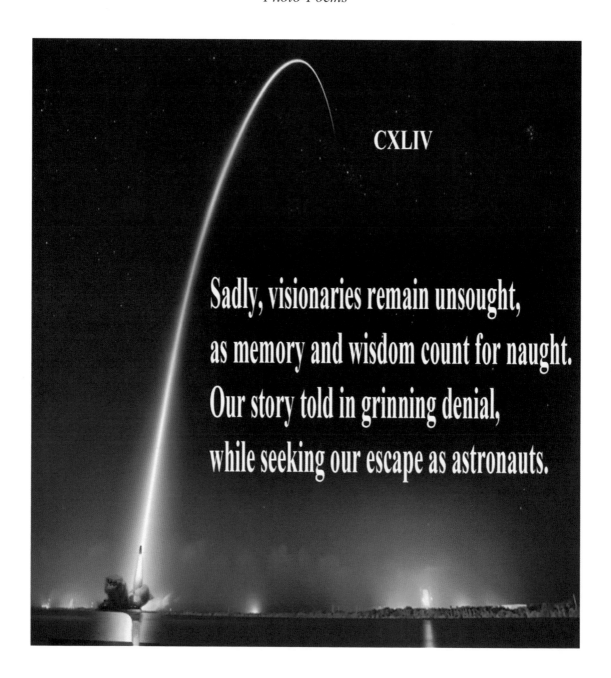

CXLIV

Sadly, visionaries remain unsought,
as memory and wisdom count for naught.
Our story told in grinning denial,
while seeking our escape as astronauts.

CXLIV

Sadly, visionaries remain unsought,

as memory and wisdom count for naught.

Our story told in grinning denial,

while seeking our escape as astronauts.

LXXVII

Upon grass I count stars—sparkling carefree,

mumbling numbers
I cannot keep, I must agree:

The earth will
keep spinning after I go,

as sky diamonds
keep twinkling

without me...

LXXVII

Upon grass I count stars—sparkling carefree,
mumbling numbers I cannot keep, I must agree:
The earth will keep spinning after I go
as sky diamonds keep twinkling without me…

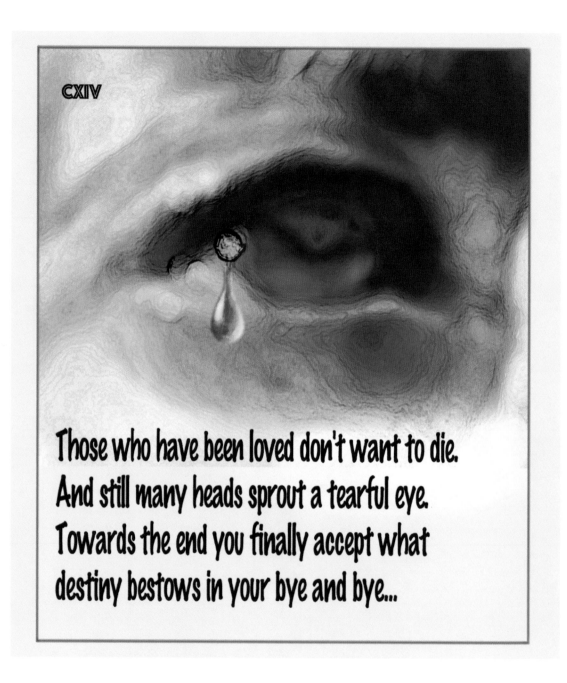

CXIV

Those who have been loved don't want to die.
And still many heads sprout a tearful eye.
Towards the end you finally accept what
destiny bestows in your bye and bye...

CXIV

Those who have been loved don't want to die.

And still many heads sprout a tearful eye.

Eventually you learn to accept what

providence bestows in your bye-and-bye.

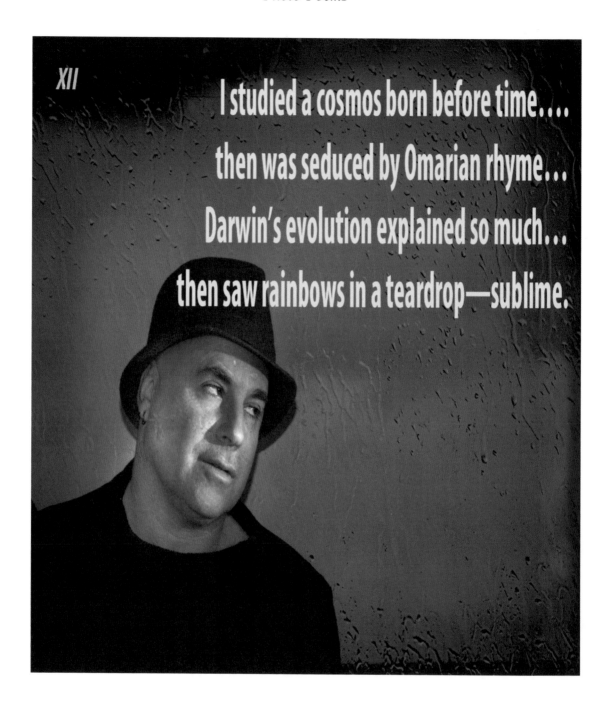

XII

I studied a cosmos born before time.....
then was seduced by Omarian rhyme...
Darwin's evolution explained so much...
then saw rainbows in a teardrop—sublime.

XII

I studied a cosmos born before time….

then was seduced by Omarian rhyme…

Darwin's evolution explained so much…

then saw rainbows in a teardrop—sublime.

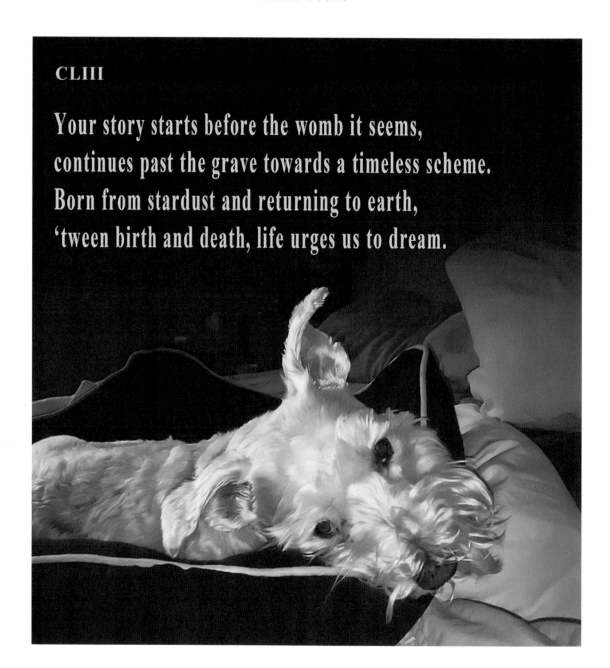

CLIII

Your story starts before the womb it seems,
continues past the grave towards a timeless scheme.
Born from stardust and returning to earth,
'tween birth and death, life urges us to dream.

CLIII

Your story starts before the womb it seems,

continues past the grave towards a timeless scheme.

Born from stardust and returning to earth,

'tween birth and death, life urges us to dream.

XCII

Asleep we soared on bright butterfly wings.
Was I dramatizing her insect schemes
or she naively performing in mine?
Does birth or death awake us from the dream?

XCII

Asleep we soared on bright butterfly wings.

Was I dramatizing her insect schemes

or she naively performing in mine?

Does birth or death awake us from the dream?

QUATRAIN CXI

Flitting like bugs in an alien's jar,
not understanding who we really are.
Some glimpse beyond the glass,
most remain blind...
The pest persists—
a trivial commissar.

CXI

Flitting like bugs in an alien's jar,

not understanding who we really are.

Some glimpse beyond the glass, most remain blind…

The pest persists—a trivial commissar.

CLVX

A careless foot finds a bug. Do they wonder?
Not grasping why, to fate they surrender.
And when the unseen broom sweeps us away
do we not also see it as fate's blunder.

Perspective

CLXI

Insects soldiering along, come and go.
Do they sense we view them so far below?
As we lofty hairless apes discuss our path,
have we reached beyond what bugs know?

CLVX

A careless foot finds a bug. Do they wonder?

Not grasping why, to fate they surrender.

And when the unseen brush sweeps us away

do we not also see it as fate's blunder.

CLXI

Insects soldiering along, come and go.

Do they sense we view them so far below?

As we lofty hairless apes discuss our path,

have we reached beyond what the bugs know?

CXXXII

Our pale blue dot barely seen in sunlight,
where chosen peoples justify their fight.
Will our insignificance teach the value
of working together in the vast dark night?

CXXXII

Our pale blue dot barely seen in sunlight,
where chosen peoples justify their fight.
Will our insignificance teach the value
of working together in the vast dark night?

XXXIV

Ah' the Camellia blooming in early Spring
falls to the ground a beautiful, lonely thing.
The color fades, the blooms blow away,
bravely leaving no imprint ...forever unseen.

XXXIV

Ah' the Camellia blooming in early Spring
falls to the ground a beautiful, lonely thing.
The color fades, the blooms blow away,
bravely leaving no imprint … forever unseen.

CIX

How has evil triumphed over our bliss?
How can we make meaning out of this?
No reason appears before my mind,
Tis the failure of our double helix.

CIX

How has evil triumphed over our bliss?

How can we make meaning out of this?

No reason appears before my mind,

Perchance the failure of our double helix.

CXXXIII

After i lay down in dark infinity,
what then becomes of this thing called me?
Then again, where was I before my birth?
My core always present, just differently.

CXXXIII

After i lay down in dark infinity,

what then becomes of this thing called me?

Then again, where was I before my birth?

My core always present, just differently.

ADIOS

The FitzOmars' many skeptical and fatalistic quatrains mirror today's loss of faith in humans, society, and the deity above. And after experiencing too many years of human and scientific "progress," my quatrains also echo these disappointments. Still, I find comfort and balance in the poets' joyful and philosophical toasts to our brief lives.

In this final chapter, I return to sip from my Omarian Martini. The recipe begins by pouring a double shot of my favorite sober-yet-smiling liquor. Then the divine bartender blends in an ounce of acceptance and shakes it up with crystalline ice. The mixologist for my soul pours it all into a golden-hued chalice, and finally tops it off with an ironic wink for the garnish.

As you imbibe your favorite beverage and the words scattered about this book, you may become filled with the urgency of seizing the day. For me the joy begins when I stand before the starry night sky and deeply inhale a spiritual awe. I become inebriated with the beauty and grandeur of our cosmos. And when the philosophical glass is drained and I've had my fill; I am more likely to notice the small, nearby, amazing scenes. These may include the delicate and complex songs of birds, the warm light reflecting off a full Harvest Moon, or dew clinging to a camellia.

In most FitzOmar books, the ending quatrains begin with draining the cup of life and then turning it over without regret. I'll end by offering you my fare-thee-well toast:

Here's to living your best life

even in the worst of times...

Bottoms up my friends.

CVI

Let's speak of the once
that was yesterday...
Stories recalled from
the gold leaf dossier.

Ignore tomorrow's
beckoning finger,
the ringing phone,
ticking clock
—we disobey

CVI

Let's speak of the once that was yesterday...
Stories recalled from the gold leaf dossier.
Ignore tomorrow's beckoning finger,
the ringing phone, ticking clock—we disobey

CLXIX

**In my experience
life is learning**

**from footfalls stumbling
and discerning;**

**seeking to evade
pitfalls that ensnare,**

**ever curious,
my soul
still yearning.**

CLXIX

In my experience life is learning
from footfalls stumbling and discerning;
seeking to evade pitfalls that ensnare,
ever curious, my soul still yearning.

CLXVII

I feel I know less today than yesterday.
A tinge of uncertainty suggests decay.
Ah but to sip confidence from a cup...
Perhaps it's the chaos theory at play.

CLXVII

I feel I know less today than yesterday.

A tinge of uncertainty suggests decay.

Ah but to sip confidence from a cup...

Perhaps it's the chaos theory at play.

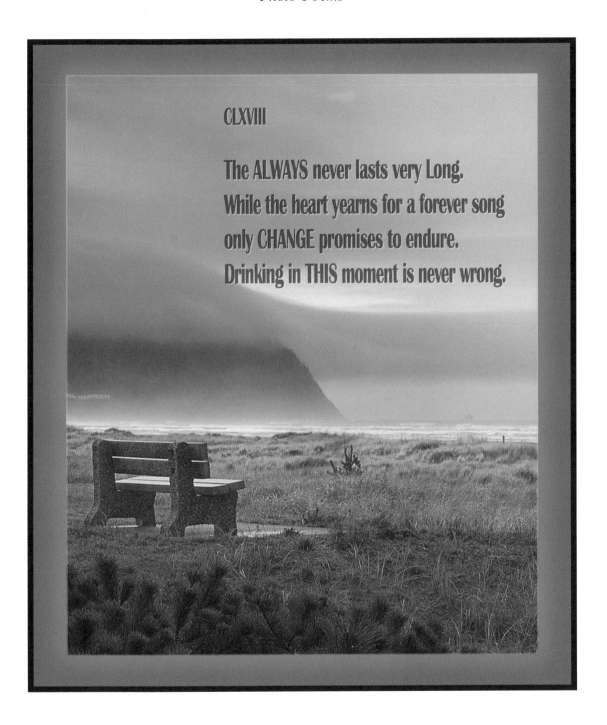

CLXVIII

The ALWAYS never lasts very Long.
While the heart yearns for a forever song
only CHANGE promises to endure.
Drinking in THIS moment is never wrong.

CLXVIII

The ALWAYS never lasts very Long.
While the heart yearns for a forever song
only CHANGE promises to endure.
Drinking in THIS moment is never wrong.

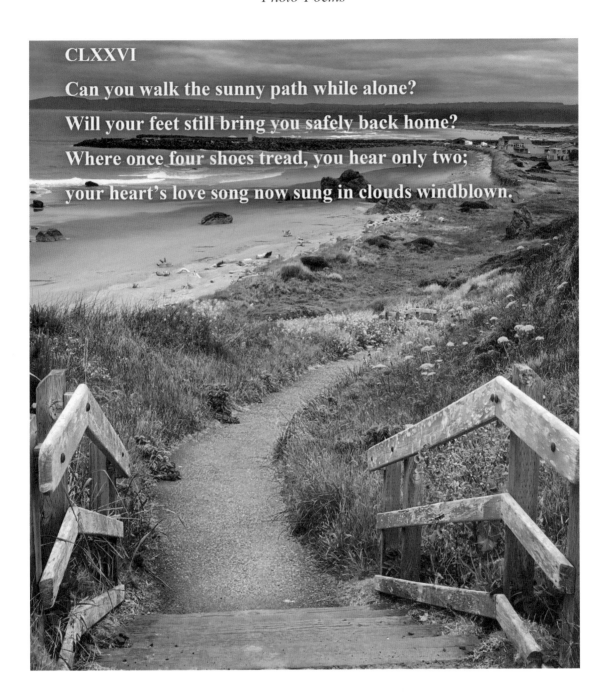

CLXXVI

Can you walk the sunny path while alone?

Will your feet still bring you safely back home?

Where once four shoes tread, you hear only two;

your heart's love song now sung in clouds windblown.

CLXXVI

Can you walk the sunny path all alone?

Will your feet still bring you safely back home?

Where once four shoes tread, you hear only two;

your heart's love song now sung in clouds windblown.

LXXVI

Blissfully cooking a gourmet meal one more time,
my life spent searching for fate's plan and rhyme.
Drained the cup; turned it over without regret…
recalling friends and drink, in love entwined.

LXXVI

Blissfully cooking a gourmet meal one more time,
my life spent searching for fate's plan and rhyme.
Drained the cup; turned it over without regret…
recalling friends and drink, in love entwined.

CLXXV

When alone can one still make a toast?

Caress the glass holding memory's ghost,

exhale, tenderly listen, and Later

join your love in the final adios...

CLXXV

When alone can one still make a toast?

Caress the glass holding memory's ghost,

exhale, tenderly listen, and later

join your love in the final adios

Martin's Other Books You Might Enjoy

Books Exploring FitzOmar Themes

Writing An Obituary Worth Reading

A Guide to Writing a Fulfilling Life-Review

My Mixology

Cocktails, Funny Tales & Literary Sleight of Hand

How To Stay In Love, Forever

...Forty-plus Years of Love Poems, Letters, and PhotoArt

Books From The FitzOmarDorf Library

Sipping From The Rubáiyát's Chalice

My Journey with The Rubáiyát of Omar Khayyám

Kibbles for the Soul

Poems About the Joy, Irony, Fatalism and Transience of Life

Photo•Poems

Living Your Best Life, Even In The Worst Of Times...

Made in the USA
Columbia, SC
26 June 2018